Designer Science

Dynamic Demonstrations that Illustrate

BOOK 1

Loren and Cheryl Petty Herbert

World rights reserved. This book or any portion thereof may not be copied or reproduced in any form or manner whatever, except as provided by law, without the written permission of the publisher, except by a reviewer who may quote brief passages in a review.

The author assumes full responsibility for the accuracy of all facts and quotations as cited in this book. The opinions expressed in this book are the author's personal views and interpretations, and do not necessarily reflect those of the publisher.

This book is provided with the understanding that the publisher is not engaged in giving spiritual, legal, medical, or other professional advice. If authoritative advice is needed, the reader should seek the counsel of a competent professional.

Copyright © 2019 Loren and Cheryl Petty Herbert

Copyright © 2019 TEACH Services, Inc.

ISBN-13: 978-1-4796-1121-8 (Paperback)

ISBN-13: 978-1-4796-1122-5 (ePub)

Library of Congress Control Number: 2019911431

Unless otherwise indicated, all Scripture quotations are from the King James Version.

The American King James Version is produced by Stone Engelbrite, a simple word for word update from the King James English.

The Christian Standard Bible. Copyright © 2017 by Holman Bible Publishers. Used by permission. Christian Standard Bible®, and CSB® are federally registered trademarks of Holman Bible Publishers, all rights reserved.

The Clear Word: An Expanded Paraphrase of the Bible to Nurture Faith and Growth. Review and Herald Pub. Association, Hagerstown, MD, 1994.

The Common English Bible (CEB). All rights reserved. *Contemporary English Version* (CEV), copyright © 1995 by American Bible Society.

GOD'S WORD®, © 1995 God's Word to the Nations. Used by permission of Baker Publishing Group.

The Holy Bible New International Version®. (NIV). Copyright © 1973, 1978, 1984 by International Bible Society. All rights reserved.

The Holy Bible, New Century Version®. (NCV). Copyright © 2005 by Thomas Nelson, Inc.

THE MESSAGE. Copyright © by Eugene H. Peterson 1993, 1994, 1995, 1996, 2000, 2001, 2002. Used by permission of Tyndale House Publishers, Inc.

New International Reader's Version. (NirV). Copyright © 1995, 1996, 1998, 2014 by Biblica, Inc.®. Used by permission. All rights reserved worldwide.

New King James Version® (NKJV), Copyright © 1982 by Thomas Nelson. Used by permission. All rights reserved.

www.TEACHServices.com • (800) 367-1844

"Loren and Cheryl Herbert came to our school in Charlotte for a Week of Prayer. Each morning they gave delightful science demonstrations that really captured the students' attention. All through the demonstrations they made spiritual applications. Students remained engaged with the presentation throughout, and they seemed to understand the lessons taught. I appreciated their focus on Jesus and His love. I certainly recommend them to any school looking for a Christ-centered and science-based series."

— J. Wendell Carlton, retired teacher

"My family and I are blessed to take in Designer Science programs at least once a month during the children's story time. We were so impressed with the presentations that Cheryl and Loren put together that we requested they do a 30-minute program for our son's birthday. The program was excellent. The demonstration of scientific principles married to spiritual lessons is an immensely effective vehicle for teaching our young people."

— David Whatton, member,
Waynesville Seventh-day Adventist Church

"At a recent Outdoor Education event at NOSOCA Pines Ranch... over 35 young people gave their hearts to Christ and requested baptism for the first time. What a joy and privilege it was to pass these names on to the local church pastors in order to follow up on nurturing these young souls for the Kingdom and leading them to baptism. We are called by God to provide these types of opportunities to instruct and lead our young people in making decisions for Him"

— Rick Anderson, Associate Director of Education/
Carolina Conference of SDA

"God's hand is clearly in this marvelous tool and His wonderful servants, Loren and Cheryl Herbert. These folks have taken the basic themes of Salvation, Prophecy, and others, and set them in the context of science experiments and fundamentals of creation science. Children, teens, and adults have been captured by the demonstrations which have led them through the door to the Creator.

I was happy watching teens in the Greenville County Juvenile Detention Center attentively watching all week in Bible Camp and then recalling God's mercy and fairness. Many, if not most of these (thieves, drug users, gang members, murderers, partying) kids are Biblically illiterate. Yet many today still recall the lessons taught. Our own kids at VBS still speak of the amazing God demonstrated in the lessons taught.

I believe the God of Creation is under greater attack than ever before. Of course, the leader of the attack knows he has a short time, so his efforts increase. What an opportunity is ours to use Scripture and Spirit of Prophecy to fight this battle. Pastors, teachers, lay members can use Creation Science in so many settings (children's stories, sermons, Sabbath School, VBS, etc.) to point to our Creator and Redeemer."

— Gerald L. Mobey, Pastor,
Greenville Seventh-day Adventist Church

Foreword

I first met the Herberts when accepting an invitation to pastor a congregation that operated a private Christian-based elementary school. Loren and Cheryl were the two main teachers. Having recently left a university environment, I was impressed of how fortunate that little school was to have such remarkable individuals in leadership.

My weekly visits to the classrooms to give a devotional—almost always illustrated with an item from nature—only increased my admiration and respect for their professionalism and willingness to serve. And that first impression has only increased during the last thirty years. There are few people who have such wide interest and extensive and diverse talent, and yet remain so humble. They epitomize what is called a "teaching ministry."

As a team, Loren and Cheryl bring the Word of God and works of God together in unique ways to illustrate and apply life lessons. Children are quickly interested and engaged in the presentations, and make positive moral decisions as a result.

You can benefit from their decades of classroom demands—their cumulative experience of how to keep the attention of children in order to teach them and guide their spiritual development. If you want practical demonstrations of spiritual truths, clearly explained, and easily adapted, then this is a resource you will want to have.

—Mark A. Heisey, SDA pastor, author, and editor of PREACH IT! Sermon Resource

Table of Contents

INTRODUCTION		10
COROLLARY 1.	**Secret Writing** (Theme: God's love) – Use phenolphthalein to write an invisible message and household ammonia to make it visible.	14
COROLLARY 2.	**Trust Me** (Theme: Trust) – Puncture a plastic bag filled with water over a volunteer's head and hopefully not get anyone wet.	17
COROLLARY 3.	**U-Turn: The Duck and Bunny** (Theme: The Changed Heart) – Use optical illusions, one illustrating perspective and the other using refraction to show a change in direction.	20
COROLLARY 4.	**Make-a-Man** (Theme: The creation of a human being) – Combine the elements of the human body and testify to the mighty power of the Creator.	25
COROLLARY 5.	**Ping-Pong Science, Floating Earth** (Theme: How God holds us up) – Illustrate Bernoulli's Principle with a blow dryer and a ping-pong ball, and also with a leaf blower and an inflatable globe.	30

Corollary 6.	**Sound Writing** (Theme: The power of words) – Show the effect of sound waves produced by your words, using a fruit can, a balloon, a broken mirror, a laser pointer, and a few other odds and ends. Lots of fun!	34
Corollary 7.	**Broken for Me** (Theme: Christ's sacrifice) – Make it look as if you can repair broken glass since the refractive index of Wesson® vegetable oil and Pyrex® are very nearly the same.	40
Corollary 8.	**He Raises Me Up** (Theme: How God raises us up) – Use an inexpensive levitation wand (available for purchase online), which is actually a mini Van de Graaff generator, to demonstrate the power to "lift up."	44
Corollary 9.	**Special Spores** (Theme: God's protection) – Dramatically illustrate the security of God's protective hand in this perennial favorite in which *Lycopodium* powder yields a lovely fireball.	49
Corollary 10.	**Let Your Light Shine** (Theme: The believer's light) – Indicate the lights of those who are present with candles of all shapes and sizes. Magnesium ribbon, when lighted, demonstrates the true Light of the world.	54

COROLLARY 11.	**Density Tower** (Theme: The importance of the Sabbath) – Carefully pour liquids of different colors and densities on top of each other to vividly illustrate the need to follow directions.	57
COROLLARY 12.	**The Long, Dark Road; the Balloon without a Bang** (Theme: Providence) – Pop a balloon when fire is applied to its surface, unless water is present to dissipate the heat. This is an illustration of God's answer to prayer.	63
COROLLARY 13.	**I Can See Clearly, Baptism** (Theme: Baptism) – Illustrate the effects of sin and Jesus' power to remove those effects. Water starts clear and colorless, turns hot pink, and then becomes clear and colorless again.	68

Introduction

Designer Science

When you buy a "designer" product, you are usually paying extra for the prestige of using a product created by someone who has proven to be the "best" in a chosen genre. What better way is there to enjoy science than to see it through the eyes of its Designer? So what better way is there to enjoy science or to begin to know the Creator than to seek understanding from the original Designer and to use demonstrations from His laws of science?

Our logo features the symbol for an atom, with a picture of the Creator for the nucleus, signifying that Christ is the Center, the Beginning and the Ending, the All-in-All, the great "I Am."

Rationale

Young and old, when presented with spiritual connections to the One who sustains His creation through universal constants, can more fully appreciate His love and care for His creatures.

The awesome Designer who made it possible for us to "live, and move, and have our being" (Acts 17:28) and then made provision for our redemption can be trusted to keep His word.

Who we are

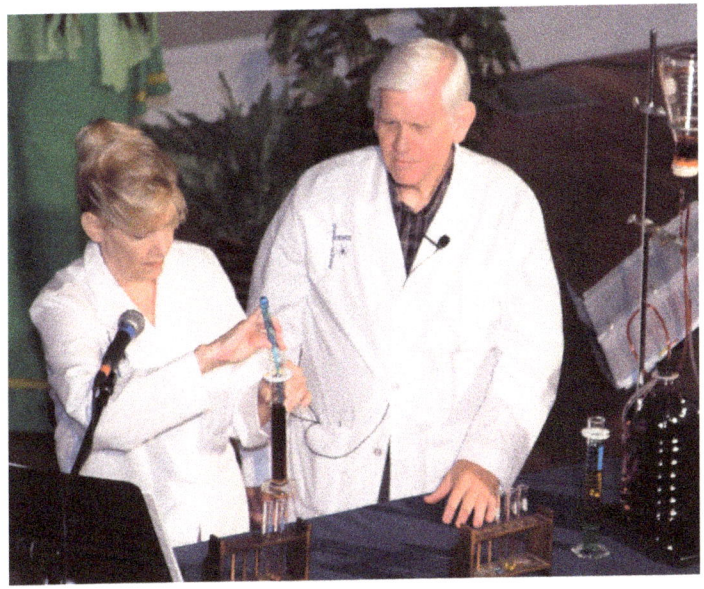

After retiring from over forty years in educational service—encompassing kindergarten through college—we knew that we needed to find another ministry and that we had to do something with the PILES of teaching materials that we had left over. So, considering that Loren's graduate degree is in science education and Cheryl's degree is in communications and math, we realized that we could collaborate to share the importance of God's love, and "Designer Science" was born.

Since beginning this ministry, we have had the opportunity to have a regular daily "Designer Science" segment in the Junior department at Carolina Camp meeting, have been featured at a Pathfinder Camporee, have presented at Vacation Bible Schools, have offered sermons, and have told children's stories, given worship talks, and have presented outdoor education features and weeks of prayer. We even spent a week in lock-down each morning in a juvenile detention center with teenagers serving time for everything from shoplifting to murder.

But, of all the experiences we have had, our favorite is probably the weeks of prayer, where we have been privileged to spend a full week watching the Holy Spirit work on precious young ones. So many who fill out cards after such events say that they are giving their hearts to Jesus for the first time or that they want to prepare for baptism.

How to use this book

This book features some of the demonstrations that we have used for sermon illustrations, worship talks, children's stories, and other presentations.

We make our presentations together. The red type is Loren's dialog and the black type is Cheryl's. Occasionally both speak in unison, and that is denoted in purple.

By having two of us presenting together it removes the necessity of calling an assistant for some of the demonstrations. Two can also keep the attention of the audience better. At least it works well for us.

Nonetheless, these demonstrations can be done by a single person doing both parts. You just need to be sure to try them out in advance, figuring out where a volunteer assistant is required.

Safety is of ultimate importance. There is no lesson that cannot be brought home in a safe way, and safety must be instilled in the minds of the audience you are reaching—especially if they are young. So, use safety glasses, have a fire extinguisher handy, and explain that you have taken special care, even though something might look exciting. Repeat the old but necessary warning: "Don't try this without your parent with you!"

There are unlimited applications of each of these demonstrations. For instance, we use phenolphthalein for

"Secret Writing" and also when we do the story of Daniel and the handwriting on the wall. We use it in talking about baptism and about Pilate's washing his hands at Jesus' trial.

We also use the Special Spores demonstration in a slightly different apparatus in the story of the Fiery Furnace. We encourage you to use your imagination, and may God bless you and your efforts.

COLOR KEY

Black: Speaker 1

Red: Speaker 2

Purple: Both Speakers together

Blue: Directions

Corollary 1

SECRET WRITING
Nature, God's Other Book

SET UP: Set the prepared poster board on an easel in front of the audience Have a spray bottle of ammonia ready for use.

"In the beginning God created the heaven and the earth."

Do you know what He created each day? Let's review.

On the first day, He created light.

On the second day, He created the firmament, or the sky.

On the third day, He created the dry land and all the plants.

On the fourth day, He created the sun, moon, and stars.

On the fifth day, He created the fish and the birds.

On the sixth day, He created the land animals and the people.

On the seventh day, God rested, blessing the seventh day and making the Sabbath for man.

What a beautiful Sabbath that must have been! Can you imagine it?

Did you know that the Sabbath was made to be a weekly birthday for our world, for all of nature? It was to remind us that Jesus created the world.

So, going out and spending time in the beauty of nature is a very special way to keep the Sabbath.

Listen to some lovely words about being out in nature:

"'God is love' is written upon every opening bud, upon the petals of every flower, and upon every spire of grass."

The lovely birds fill the air with their happy songs; the delicate flowers perfume the air; the lofty trees color the forest with their rich foliage of living green.

"Though the curse of sin has caused the earth to bring forth thorns and thistles, there are flowers on the thistles, and the thorns are hidden by roses.

"All things in nature testify to the tender, fatherly care of our God, and how He wants to make His children happy" (E. G. White, *Christian Education*, p. 67).

Point to the picture of the flower petals.

Oh, did God write secret messages to us on flower petals?

We may not be able to see the letters that spell the message,

but, in the beauty of the flowers, the message is clear.

Spray the poster board, and the message "God is love" appears.

Ah-h-h, that's the message of the flowers. So, every time we hear a bird sing,

or smell a flower, or see a sunset,

or enjoy anything in nature,

we should remember that ...

"God is love."

PREPARATION

Supplies:

1. Household ammonia
2. Phenolphthalein 1% (available for purchase online)
3. Spray bottle that can produce a fine mist
4. Small paint sponges or cotton swabs
5. White poster board
6. Easel

Directions:

1. Draw a large, simple outline pencil drawing of a flower like this:

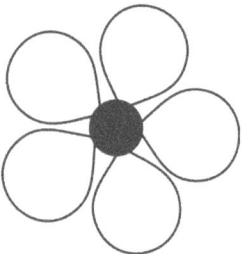

2. On each petal write, "God is love," using a sponge or a cotton swab dipped in phenolphthalein. Make sure to soak the paper thoroughly; then let it dry.
3. Fill the spray bottle with ammonia.
4. Display the pencil drawing of the flower during your talk, and follow the directions given in the narration. (Don't over spray, or it will run. However, you need to spray enough, or it will disappear too fast. If it does disappear, you can spray it again to make it reappear.)
5. Be sure to do a small test run at home first.

Corollary 2

TRUST ME

SET UP: On a table in front of the audience, set out a pitcher with about a quart of water, a shower cap, a bath towel, a large empty bowl, a quart zip-lock freezer bag, and four or five hexagonal (not round) pencils that have been sharpened to a very sharp point.

Have you ever had someone say, "Trust me"?

Usually that means that the person is going to do something that looks dangerous or risky.

Or maybe they use those words because they have done things in the past that were not very trustworthy.

Maybe they haven't always been honest with you, so you don't know whether you can trust them or not.

Would you trust someone who would steal from you?

We all want others to trust us.

What if no one ever trusted you?

What if no one ever believed anything you said?

What if, every time something got lost at school, all your classmates wanted to search your backpack?

Well, Jesus gave us the eighth commandment to help us be trustworthy.

Who knows what the eighth commandment says?

That's right, it says: "Thou shalt not steal."

Okay, well, we don't have a demonstration about stealing—but we do have one that is called "Trust Me."

We need a helper who will trust us.

Choose a volunteer. Put a shower cap on the volunteer and place a towel around the volunteer's shoulders, while chatting about, "I hope this works," the reasons for the precautions, and especially why you asked, "Are you sure you trust me?"

Pour the water into the quart-sized baggie about ¾ full, and then zip the baggie securely.

Hold the baggie over the volunteer's head and insert the pencils, one at a time, poking completely through both sides of the baggie.

Put the baggie with the pencils still inserted into a bowl and thank the volunteer for demonstrating the concept of trust.

Aren't we glad that Jesus gave us guidelines in His law of love that will help us be trustworthy?

If we keep God's laws and our friends know that we would never steal or lie or cheat, then they will know that they can trust us!

I'm so glad that I have a Savior I can trust to love me,

and care for me,

Today …

and always!

PREPARATION

Supplies:

1. Pitcher with about a quart of water
2. Shower cap
3. Bath towel
4. Large empty bowl
5. Quart-sized zip-lock freezer bag
6. Four or five hexagonal (<u>not round</u>) pencils, sharpened very sharp

Directions:

Follow the directions within the script.

Illustration:

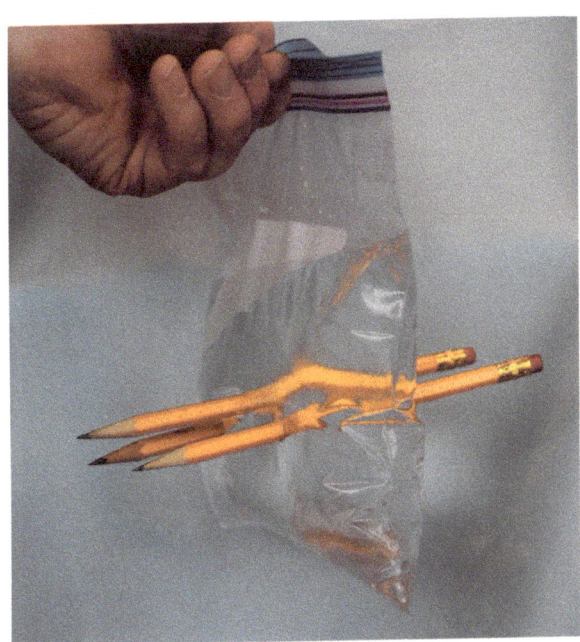

Corollary 3

H₂O U-TURN
The Duck and Bunny

SET UP: *On a presentation table place: (1) a round, clear, vertical, glass cylinder (as large as possible) filled with water, (2) a side view drawing of Saul walking (use card stock), (3) the duck/rabbit picture. Just below the surface of the table, place a* BRIGHT WORK LIGHT, *with a remote switch, aimed at the eye level of the audience.*

Today we are going to talk about two men who were really one.

Though one man, thanks to Jesus, he had a "do over" in his life.

His name was Saul.

And his name was Paul!

He was so different after meeting Jesus that even his name was changed!

You see, Saul was a very dedicated young man who sincerely wanted to serve God.

He was the star student of Gamaliel, who was the most respected professor in all Israel.

U-Turn: The Duck and Bunny ◆ 21

The religious leaders had great hopes and plans for him!

He was so on fire for his religion that he devoted his entire life to stamping out those "rotten followers of Jesus, the One who was called Christ."

The only problem was that he had spent all his time studying about his religion but not learning to know God.

He even held the coats of those who stoned Stephen, one of Jesus' most loyal followers, giving them his authorization.

But it seemed that he had done such a good job of persecuting the followers of Jesus in Jerusalem that they had fled to other locations.

So, he found himself traveling, with all his entourage, down the road to Damascus, to arrest those who had fled **or even to do worse**.

But, suddenly …

Shine the bright light directly at the audience for three to four seconds.

a dazzling light from above knocked him off his horse, and he lay looking up into what seemed an opening into heaven!

HE SAW JESUS!

That's when he did an abrupt about face in his life!

Show the picture of Saul, then lower it behind the large cylinder of water and pass it across behind the cylinder. Saul will appear to change directions. Be sure to practice this before the presentation, for Saul can sometimes be a bit unruly!

For the rest of his life he was a passionately dedicated soldier in the army of Christ!

"But," I can just hear you saying, "Saul didn't even love Jesus at first! Why did Jesus pick him?"

Remember, the Bible tells us that the LORD sees not as man sees, for man looks on the outward appearance, but the LORD looks on the heart.

Hold up picture to look like duck, and then turn it to show the rabbit.

Jesus could see Saul's heart. He saw that Saul was so devoted to what he thought was right that he would be just as committed to the genuine truth when he learned it.

Jesus knew the strength and power that this man would bring to his work when he was turned around.

So, what are some of the things we learn from the story of Paul who had been Saul?

Well, one thing we learn is that no matter how much you know ABOUT the Bible and about God, it doesn't do much good unless you KNOW AND LOVE Him.

Another thing we learn is that no matter how bad you have been, Jesus still wants you to turn around and be a worker for Him.

And a third thing we learn is that we can't see what God sees when we look at someone, so we should leave all judging to Him.

PREPARATION

Supplies:

1. Presentation table
2. Bright work light
3. Remote switch or an assistant to operate the light
4. Duck/rabbit picture on card stock. This image is all over the Internet and called the "duck/rabbit illusion." It is public domain. Look for one with a high resolution and print it on card stock.
5. Round, clear, vertical, glass cylinder (as large as possible) filled with water
6. Side-view drawing of Saul walking, glued on card stock (see next page)

Directions:

1. Set up the presentation table with a light that can shine very brightly sitting even with the surface of the table and aimed at the audience.
2. Place the cylinder of water where it can be seen by all and have the two pictures handy.

Corollary 4

MAKE-A-MAN

SET UP: On a presentation table, place: (1) the equation poster, (2) a large opaque storage tub containing (a) the specified model skeleton, (b) a large mixing spoon, and (c) three food storage containers (two empty and one containing all elements listed in "Supplies"). *This demonstration definitely needs two presenters, and it is written that way.*

King David wrote in Psalm 139, "I will give thanks to You because I have been so amazingly and miraculously made" (God's Word® Translation).

But what are we made of?

The Bible says God took the dust of the ground and created man. He administered the first anesthesia and performed the first surgery to take one of Adam's ribs to make Eve.

But what was IN that dust? What are the components of the human body?

Well, if we know the ingredients—what we are made of— can we make a man?

Well, we might not end up with a complete man because we don't have QUITE all the elements—some of the most minor ones are missing!

But let's try!

You call out the ingredients, and I'll add them to the mix.

Pull the container of elements out of the opaque tub, being careful not to expose anything else to the audience. Surreptitiously separate the two empty containers still within the opaque tub, so that the H_2O can go in one without contaminating the other elements. The assistant calls out these major elements.

Let's add our hydrogen and oxygen together because—what happens when we have two atoms of hydrogen bonded with one atom of oxygen? We get H_2O!

That's right – water! And our bodies are 75% oxygen and hydrogen.

Pour at least a cup of water into one of the empty containers. You will not use this container again in this demonstration. We use bottled water for convenience.

Next we put in some carbon. This charcoal is a form of carbon, so we will throw that in.

*Put the charcoal and all the remaining items in the **dry container**, as the assistant calls out their name.*

Next, let's add the nitrogen.

Most of the air we breathe is made up of nitrogen, so let's just scoop it in!

Add nitrogen by using hands and arms in large scooping motions to shovel the air into the opaque tub.

And then we have calcium.

Right, and calcium gives us strong bones and strong teeth, so let's use a lot of that!

Dump in a very liberal amount of calcium caplets.

And these lentils, which are high in phosphorus,

> *Add phosphorus.*

potassium,

> *Add potassium.*

sulfur,

> *Add sulfur.*

sodium and chlorine. What do we know about a common combination of sodium and chlorine?

> *Hold up the salt container.*

Yes, of course, salt!

> *Add the salt.*

Just a couple more here. Magnesium,

> *Add the magnesium.*

Now let's add two of the trace elements—copper and iron. There is enough iron in the average body to make one three-inch nail.

> *Drop in the copper and the iron.*

So, let's stir this all up and see what we get.

> *Pretend to stir vigorously, and then slowly pull out the model skeleton while saying:*

Oops! Something seems to be missing! Maybe we got TOO much calcium!

But, no, we know we were just pretending to make a man, because only God can create life.

Well, we each have a skeleton—along with arteries, veins, blood, muscles, nerves, organs, and so on.

The Bible tells us that after God formed man, He breathed into him the breath of life, and that is when the miracle happened—man became a living soul. Hallelujah!

All right, students, what was the equation we just talked about! The body plus the breath of life equals a living soul.

Hold up the poster of the equation.

Scientists have taken the equivalent amounts of elements that are in our bodies and calculated what the value of a body would be if it were broken down into its elemental components. Would you believe? It would only be $1.00!

But just compare the value of a person after God stepped in. What is the value of the living soul?

Romans 5:8 says that Jesus died for our sins. So, the value of a living soul is the life of Jesus, which He freely gave for us on the cross.

Optional ending 1:

Would someone like to pray and thank Jesus for creating us and then re-creating us?

Optional ending 2:

Today we are celebrating the Lord's Supper,

which reminds us of Jesus' great sacrifice so that we can be re-created.

Only the One who created us has the power to re-create us.

Would someone like to pray and thank Jesus for creating us and re-creating us?

PREPARATION

Supplies:

1. Poster: The Body + The Breath = The Living Soul
2. Large opaque tote (tub)
3. Three plastic storage containers, about ½ gallon
4. Realistic articulated 18-inch (45-cm.) skeleton, which is available online for $12–15
5. Large mixing spoon
6. Bottled water
7. Carbon (charcoal briquette)
8. Nitrogen (in the air)
9. Phosphorus (small bag of lentils)
10. Sulfur (order online)
11. Sodium and chlorine (round box of salt—make sure it is recognizable for the audience)
12. Copper (such as, a copper strap, a pre-1982 penny, or a small piece of copper pipe)
13. Iron (nail)

   We found the following elements in the vitamin and mineral displays in the health and beauty aisle:

14. Calcium caplets
15. Potassium capsules
16. Magnesium supplements

Directions:

Follow the directions within the script.

Corollary 5

PING-PONG SCIENCE
Floating Earth

***SET UP:** On a presentation table, place a blow dryer, a ping-pong ball, a leaf blower, an inflatable globe, and a sword.*

Our verse this morning is John 3:8.

"The wind blows where it wants, and you hear the sound thereof, but can not tell from where it comes, and where it goes: so is every one that is born of the Spirit" (*American King James Version*).

In the Bible, wind represents the Holy Spirit, who is God just like Jesus and the Father. We are going to use this blow dryer to make the wind to illustrate how God supports and cares for us.

Hold up blow dryer.

And this ping-pong ball will be us.

Hold up the ping-pong ball facing the audience.

See, we're smiling!

Ping-Pong Science, Floating Earth ◆ 31

Demonstrate by first turning on the blow dryer, holding it down low and aiming it straight up. Next, center the ping-pong ball within the stream of wind and release it. (PRACTICE FIRST!)

Now suppose we decided that we could just take care of ourselves. We are big enough and strong enough ...

That's what Peter thought in the garden just before Jesus was captured.

He whipped out his sword to protect the Son of God!

Pick up and swing the sword.

What was he thinking? We can't protect God! He protects us!

But Peter wanted to depend on his sword rather than praying and having faith that God would do what was best. And look how well that sword could support and care for us.

Hold up the ball and try to balance it on the sword.

Jesus told Peter, "Put away your sword, for those who live by the sword will die by the sword" (Matt. 26:52, version unknown).

Now God has more to do than just take care of you and me. He is responsible for the whole universe!

And our earth, as big as it seems to us, is just a small part of the universe.

Isn't it wonderful to know that He has the whole world under His care?

Repeat the ping-pong science demonstration, this time using the leaf blower and the inflatable globe.

At times it seems that this world is out of control, with hurricanes, tornados, floods, shootings at schools, in the streets, and at churches, explosions and other terrorist activities and wars. But God is in control of our world and is holding and guiding it!

These demonstrations today were possible because of another of the Designer's laws of physics called "Bernoulli's principle." It was discovered by a man, but it was created by God.

Let's bow our heads. Our Father, thank You for protecting us and holding us up. We love You. Amen.

Ping-Pong Science, Floating Earth ◆ 33

PREPARATION

Supplies:

1. Presentation table
2. Blow dryer – Find a blow dryer with the longest nozzle and strongest, most concentrated, stream of air possible.
3. Ping-pong ball – This needs to be a ping-pong ball with a yellow "smiley face."
4. Leaf blower – Electric (NOT gas!) – You may need an extension nozzle. You can use a cardboard tube if necessary.
5. Inflatable globe – a 12-inch to 16-inch globe (as a beach ball) is available for purchase online and through a school supply.
6. Sword – Be creative, a real sword or homemade one covered with aluminum foil!

Directions:

Follow the directions within the script.

Illustration:

Corollary 6

SOUND WRITING ON THE WALL

SET UP: On a display table, place an arrow, a silver-colored bowl of golden delicious apples, and the laser/peach-can/balloon/mirror apparatus. Have a screen or a semi smooth, light colored wall available at some distance – the farther you place it, the larger your demonstration will be.

Today we have two verses for you.

King David, in Psalms 64:2, 3, prayed:

"Protect me from the plots of the wicked and from the traps of evil men" (The Clear Word).

"They sharpen their tongues like swords and aim their words like deadly arrows" (New International Version).

Hold up the arrow.

And David's son, King Solomon, in Proverbs 25:11, said:

"The right word spoken at the right time is as beautiful as gold apples in a silver bowl" (*New Century Version*).

Point to the bowl of apples.

There is a little poem I like, and it says:

> Boys flying kites haul in their white winged birds;
> You can't do that when you're flying words.
> "Careful with fire," is good advice, we know:
> "Careful with words," is ten times doubly so.
> —Will Carleton, "The First Settler's Story"

Repeat two times, and then have the children repeat the words with you.

If you say something, can you see your words? Even though you can't SEE the words you speak, they can be powerful for either good or bad. They can make other people feel happy or sad. Who can tell me some words that might make someone feel sad? Now what are some words to make someone feel glad?

Today we are going to have a chance to see our words—in a manner of speaking.

But first we must understand a little bit about how our Designer so cleverly created the science of sound.

Our speech produces sound waves in the air …

Wave hand through the air from mouth outward.

which strike the balloon stretched at the end of this can.

Hold up the can and point to the balloon.

These waves cause the balloon membrane to vibrate.

When our laser beam strikes the vibrating mirror that is attached to the balloon …

Show the piece of mirror on the balloon, and then clip the binder clip on the laser pointer to turn it on. Be very careful not to point the laser toward anyone's eyes.

the vibrations become visible when they are reflected back to the screen.

Demonstrate by saying different words and sounds into the opening of the can opposite the balloon. Put can completely over mouth. Experiment with different words, pitches, volumes, etc. We have found that a deep male voice usually has a larger range, but not always. Explosive words, such as "POP," seem to do well. Going through the vowel sounds usually is fun. If you are brave, let your audience try—without any mouth contact with the apparatus.

In this way, we can see the way that vibrations come from our words, but we cannot see the effects our words have on the feelings of others.

Our words can stab our friends like an arrow,

Hold up the arrow.

or they can be as beautiful as a silver bowl full of golden apples!

Point to the bowl of apples.

Let's all promise, with Jesus' help, to use only words that will honor Jesus and help others.

PREPARATION

Supplies:

1. Archery arrow
2. Silver-colored bowl
3. Golden delicious apples
4. Green laser pointer – a red pointer will work if the room is very dark, but a green laser pointer, being far stronger, is highly recommended for this demonstration.
5. 29-ounce peach can (or the can of any other fruit or vegetable)
6. Paint stirrer – usually free from Lowe's, Ace, Home Depot, etc.
7. Several 12-inch balloons (in case of breakage during assembly)
8. Duct tape
9. Ten heavy rubber bands (you need six, the rest are spares in case of breakage)
10. One clothes pin
11. One paper clip
12. Small mirror
13. Double-sided scotch tape
14. One large binder clip

Directions:

1. Place silver-colored bowl of golden delicious apples on the table. (These can be given to the children at the close of the story.)
2. Get a can of peaches, 29 oz., eat the peaches, and cut both ends out of the can. Wash and dry the can.

3. Take a 12-inch balloon, cut off the open end just where the tube opens to the round part of the balloon so you can stretch the balloon tightly over one end of the can and secure it with duct tape, if necessary. Usually the balloon will hold on its own.

4. Take a small mirror (approximately 1/2-inch square) and attach it to the middle of the stretched balloon. (From personal experience, we can say, if you need to break a mirror from an old compact, it will not bring bad luck.) A piece of double-sided scotch tape will work to hold the mirror in place. Hold your thumb against the balloon from inside the can while pressing the mirror securely from the outside.

5. Attach the can to one end of the paint stirrer using rubber bands.

6. On the other end of the paint stirrer, mount a laser pointer on a clothespin, aimed at the mirror. Use rubber bands for this also. Slide a paper clip under the wide end of the clothespin to help center the beam on the mirror. (Adjust, adjust, and adjust until it works.). Project the reflected beam on a bare wall or screen. The laser is held in the "on" position with a binder clip. **BE VERY CAREFUL THAT THE LASER IS NEVER IN A POSITION TO SHINE IN ANYONE'S EYES!**

7. Speak directly into the open end of the can, with your mouth as far into the can as possible and watch the pattern of light gyrations on the wall or screen. Experiment ahead of time, varying words, sounds, distance, and volume.

Illustrations:

Where to cut the balloon so it can stretch over the can.

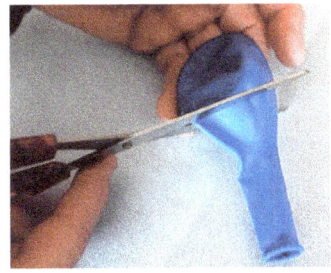

Apparatus not turned on. (Notice the switch is on the side of the laser pointer so the binder clip will press it when attached.)

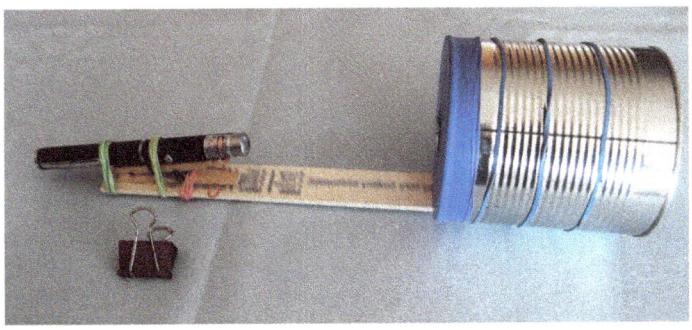

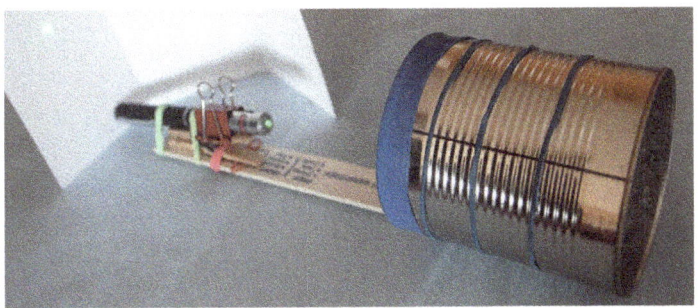

Corollary 7

BROKEN FOR ME
Communion

SET UP: On the presentation table, set out: a large clear, glass salad or mixing bowl that is ¾ full of Wesson® vegetable oil with first test tube (unbroken) already submerged in the oil, making sure the bubbles have time to disperse so that it completely disappears.

Next, lay out: a second 6-inch test tube, a square of freezer paper large enough to wrap a 6-inch test tube, and tongs.

Now lay out the crown of thorns (under a paper to hide it until use), a short-handled sledgehammer, and three very large nails.

On a tall microphone stand with the boom extended straight up, behind where you will be presenting, hang a clothes hanger with a long piece of purple fabric (we use satin) to look like a robe.

We have a Bible verse to read this morning.

First Corinthians 11, verses 23 and 24, says, "The Lord Jesus the same night in which he was betrayed took bread:

Broken for Me ◆ 41

And when He had given thanks, He brake it, and said, Take, eat: this is my body, which is broken for you: this do in remembrance of me."

This was Paul, talking about the Last Supper, when Jesus gave us the communion service that we are going to celebrate today.

Let's take a look at what was just about to happen to Jesus when He said this.

That very night, and through the next day, He was beaten repeatedly;

parts of His beard were yanked out;

He had vicious thorns smashed into His head, gouging His skin;

Lift the crown, show it, and then hang it above the robe.

He was slashed with a whip of many strands, each of which had pieces of sharp glass, metal, and bone to slice His flesh;

He had nails pounded through His hands and feet.

Hold up the nails and the sledgehammer.

And then the cross He was on was lifted to be plunged into a hole in the ground.

His heart broke.

He died.

A spear was plunged into His side.

But why would Jesus let them do this to Him?

Because we have sinned and would not be able to live forever with Jesus if the perfect Creator didn't pay the perfect price for our sins.

And although no bones were broken, that was truly a broken body; broken for you and me.

Hold up the test tube, wrap it in freezer paper, break the test tube with the sledge and show it to the audience.

That is what we will be remembering today.

Slide the broken test tube into the Wesson® oil from the paper.

But even though this seems so sad, it is also a reason for joy.

Because that broken body was made new through resurrection.

Since He was willing to let His body be broken, He assured eternal life for you and me, if we will accept His wonderful gift.

Use the tongs to pull the complete unbroken test tube out of the oil and show it to the audience.

Will we accept this sacrifice?

Who will pray for us today?

PREPARATION

Supplies:

1. Presentation table
2. Two Pyrex® or Kimax® 6-inch test tubes with no markings on them. Pyrex® kitchenware is not made of borosilicate since 1998, but lab ware still is. This demonstration works because borosilicate and Wesson® vegetable oil have the same refractive index. (We had to file off a blue patch, made for writing on the test tube, before this demonstration.)
3. Wesson® Vegetable Oil
4. Large clear glass salad bowl or mixing bowl
5. Freezer paper or other heavy paper
6. "Crown of thorns," or long thorns found in nature. We ordered a "crown of thorns" online. We have no way of knowing if it is anything like Jesus' crown, but it looks authentic.
7. Four yards of purple fabric
8. Large padded clothes hanger
9. Microphone stand with a boom
10. Short-handled sledge
11. Three very large nails, preferably spike type, old and rusty

Directions:

1. Follow the directions within the script.
2. Other Pyrex® lab ware works as well, or perhaps better, but is more expensive. We have done it with beakers, and that looks great, but test tubes are a lot less expensive.

Corollary 8

HE RAISES ME UP

SET UP: On presentation table, place the wand and the foil butterfly.

We have two Bible verses to read this morning.

Psalm 41:10 says, "But Thou, O Lord, be merciful unto me, and raise me up."

Hosea 6:2 says, "He will raise us up so we can live in His presence" (*Christian Standard Bible*).

We remember stories in the Bible in which Jesus raised people up.

He raised Peter from the stormy water. The disciples were in a boat in the middle of the sea when a storm arose. The boat was in danger of going down and they would all drown!

Then suddenly they saw a strange and eerie sight. It seemed that, through the rain and mist, they could see a Man out on top of the water, without a boat, walking toward them in the middle of the sea! Then Jesus called to them, identifying Himself, and told them not to be afraid. Yet, it was still so strange!

So, Peter had an idea. "IF IT IS REALLY YOU," HE SAID, "LET ME COME TO MEET YOU." That was typical Peter! Always speaking first and thinking later!

He Raises Me Up ◆ 45

So, when Jesus said, "COME!" Over the side of the boat Peter stepped, maybe a LITTLE hesitantly at first, but with his eyes glued on Jesus.

Isn't that how we should step out in everything we do? Say it with me, "with our eyes glued on Jesus."

But soon Peter began to think, "Hey, I'm lookin' pretty good! I'm out here walkin' on water! None of my friends have ever done that, I wonder if they realize how great I am?"—or something like that. And instantly he began to sink!

"LORD, SAVE ME!" Peter yelled. And that's when Jesus immediately reached down and lifted him up.

The first time we hear about Elijah in the Bible, he pops up standing before King Ahab and gives him a message that sounded quite rude! Elijah said, There will be no rain or even dew until I say so! And King Ahab was not known to be a very sweet and easy-going man!

Elijah faced King Ahab again on the mountain when he challenged the priests of the false god Baal to pray for rain, and then Elijah prayed at God's altar. Do you remember what happened there?

Hundreds and hundreds of prophets of Baal danced and sang and prayed and cut themselves and tried to start their fire on their altars to Baal, there on the mountaintop. All day they kept it up—to no avail.

Then it was Elijah's turn. To make sure no one could say he was cheating, he had twelve barrels of water hauled in and poured over his sacrifice. Then he prayed his simple prayer, and fire fell from heaven and burned up not only the sacrifice but also the wood on the altar and the stones that the altar was built from, and then it lapped up the water that was in the trench around the altar! WOW!

Then when Elijah saw a tiny cloud, he ran and grabbed the lead bridles on the horses pulling Ahab's chariot, and, in the deluge that followed, led the King safely down the mountain and back to his palace gate.

Elijah was used by God to give messages to a king, to raise a dead boy, and to destroy false prophets. He was even fed by birds! But when it came time for his life on earth to end, God had something extra special spectacular in store for him! A fiery chariot came swooping down and scooped him up into the clouds and on into heaven.

There were many others who were sick, sad, sinful, lame, blind and even dead, who were raised.

But these verses are talking about raising us up from sin,

or sadness,

or sickness.

In our experiment today, we are going to raise a pretend butterfly without touching it.

Of course, this is NOT the way Jesus raises us up, but it can make us think about how much Jesus loves us and wants to raise us up to be with Him.

Follow the directions on your wand using one of the "butterfly" pieces. You only need to hold the "on" button for about three seconds at a time. Make sure that there is no breeze blowing (even that of an air conditioner) where you are demonstrating. Explain that the wand has a little Van de Graaff generator inside that causes it to become statically charged—just like when you rub your feet on a carpet and touch a doorknob, or when the weather is very dry and your hair wants to stand on end. Warning: if this is a children's story, they will all want to try it. Use your discretion.

The charge on the wand and the charge on the butterfly are the same, and like charges repel. That's why the butterfly floats. However, with Jesus, we are raised up because He attracts us!

Let's pray. Thank You, Jesus, for raising me up from my sins, my temptations, my sicknesses, and my hurts. Thank you most of all for coming soon to raise me up to heaven to be with you forever. Amen.

PREPARATION

Supplies:

Flying Toy Wand by Wandarama (Amazon Prime 2/$11) or Fun Fly Stick by Unitech Toys (Online $12) Levitation Wand (Google) These are inexpensive science toys that can be used for spiritual applications.

Directions:

Follow the directions within the script, and PRACTICE.

COROLLARY 9

SPECIAL SPORES*

SET UP: On the presentation table, place four "arrows," a butane lighter, and a container of Lycopodium. *It is highly recommended that you and your assistant wear safety glasses and lab coats. Have a fire extinguisher visible and ready for use.*

We have three short verses this morning. The first is Genesis 2:7.

"Then the Lord God took dust from the ground and formed a man from it…" (*New Century Version*).

The next is Psalm 20:6.

"Now I know the Lord … saves him with his strong right hand" (New Century Version).

And, finally, the third is Ephesians 6:16:

"Above all, carry the shield of faith so that you can extinguish the flaming arrows of the evil one" (*Common English Bible*).

Who knows the three things that are needed to have fire, also called combustion? That's right: fuel, oxygen, and heat (or ignition temperature)!

Lycopodium is a club moss that produces spores, which are like seeds, in ferns. These spores are very flammable, but they clump together so closely that oxygen can't get in between them.

Pick up the bottle of Lycopodium and pour a generous amount into your non-dominant hand.

When you apply the heat by jabbing a flaming match into a pile of spores, it won't keep burning because of a lack of oxygen. But when the spores leave the hand, they spread out, and each spore is surrounded by air that is full of oxygen, and then you better watch out!

These dust-like particles I am holding represent you and me. God made us out of the dust of the ground.

We are all grouped close together in GOD'S STRONG HAND. What better place is there to be?

How can we stay close together? Maybe by going to Sabbath School and church. Maybe by going to church school. For some, who only have their mom or dad, it is by huddling with them in GOD'S STRONG HAND.

Satan is trying to get at us. He is shooting his flaming arrows at us. What can those arrows be? They may be temptations.

Sometimes we are tempted to lose our temper or to use bad words, but if we keep close together in GOD'S STRONG HAND, we are safe.

You hold the first "arrow" and light it from the butane lighter your assistant is holding for you. Immediately drive the flaming end into the pile of Lycopodium powder in your hand, making sure that it is in the powder deeply enough to snuff out the fire.

Maybe we are tempted to tell lies or to cheat in school. Maybe we like to say bad things about other people because we think it makes us look better.

Do the second "arrow" the same as the first.

Maybe we are tempted to doubt that God could love us.

Follow the same with the third "arrow."

You see? Every arrow that the evil one shot at us was extinguished!

Oh, but look what happens if we leave God's strong hand when we decide that we don't need His protection!

*Making sure you have stepped several feet back from everyone else, hold the hand with Lycopodium fully extended from your body and just above head level. Directly below the Lycopodium hand, just below waist level, have the dominant hand holding the flaming "arrow." Opening fingers rapidly from bottom to the top so the Lycopodium powder falls in a thick cloud, **not** all as one clump, **not** slowly in a thin stream, and **not** widely scattered. Be prepared to step back! Definitely practice, practice, practice!)*

So, let's determine today that we are going to stay in—say it with me—HIS STRONG RIGHT HAND!

---

* *We give special thanks to our dear friend Elder Mark Heisey for this demonstration.*

PREPARATION

Supplies:

1. Four homemade "arrows"
2. 11-inch butane lighter
3. Airtight bottle of *Lycopodium clavatum* (available for purchase online)
4. Two pairs of safety glasses
5. Lab coat
6. Fire extinguisher
7. Large trash bag

Directions:

1. This demonstration definitely needs two presenters.
2. To make "arrows," you will use large fireplace matches. They are longer, thicker, and easier to properly cut. For the "feathers" of the arrows, cut feather shapes from four different colored note cards – two feathers of each color. Make a slice into the end of each match and insert two of the cut outs, folding them slightly, and your "flaming arrows" are ready. See illustrations.
3. Use the large trash bag as a drop cloth by opening it with scissors and spreading it in an open spot where you will be doing your final demonstration. Some of the spores won't burn and will fall to the floor. While they do no harm, if you don't use a drop cloth, they will need to be vacuumed up.
4. Make sure to have enough *Lycopodium* to do a second try in case the first one is a "fizzle." In our experience, the first attempt may not be satisfactory.

Illustrations:

Corollary 10

LET YOUR LIGHT SHINE

Arrange candles all over the presentation table, placing the ring stand with clamped coil of magnesium ribbon in the center and raised a little higher than the highest candle. Place a butane lighter on the table and have a fire extinguisher available. Wear safety glasses for this demonstration.

Jesus said, "Let your light so shine before men, that they may see your good works, and glorify your Father in heaven" (Matt. 5:16).

These candles represent our church.

You know—the church members here in our town.

This one can be our pastor.

Oh, yes, we do come in all shapes and sizes!

And we even have some children here.

We can't forget the children!

How can they …

Wave hand over all candles.

… let their lights shine? Maybe the pastor lets his light shine by preaching the sermon today.

Have the audience list ways that the lights can shine, and light candles as ideas come from them. Depending on the number of candles you use, you may need to light more than one candle at each suggestion for time's sake.

Okay, that is a lot of ways to let our lights shine.

Those are a lot of good works!

But all these things will not make us ready to go to heaven with Jesus when He comes; they will not save us.

No, we are saved only by knowing Jesus and accepting His love and sacrifice for us.

But IF we love Him, we will WANT to do the good works He calls us to do. And just look how brightly these good works shine!

Now let's compare our good works with just one look at Jesus.

Light the magnesium with the butane lighter. It takes a few seconds to ignite. Wait while it burns.

If we trust our own goodness, there isn't much hope.

Our good works are important only because they show our love for Jesus.

This love we give back to HIM because He loved us first.

Jesus said, "If I be lifted up, I will draw all men unto me" (John 12:32).

Where was Jesus lifted up?

Wait for an answer.

That's right, on the cross.

We accept Jesus' perfect life and death in place of our feeble flame and look always to Him.

Who will pray for us today?

56 ◆ *Designer Science*

PREPARATION

Supplies:

1. As many different candles as you can find—two or three birthday candles, a tea light, a pillar candle, a votive candle, a taper candle, a candle in a container, etc. Make sure you have different sizes, colors, shapes, and brightness. Be sure that you can safely light them without fear of an accident. You can place them all in a large flat box of sand if there is concern.
2. Laboratory-quality ring stand with a test tube clamp (or equivalent) to hold the magnesium.
3. 11-inch butane lighter
4. Magnesium ribbon coiled with increasing diameter at the bottom. See illustration.
5. Fire extinguisher
6. Safety glasses

Directions:

Use directions included in the narrative.

Illustration:

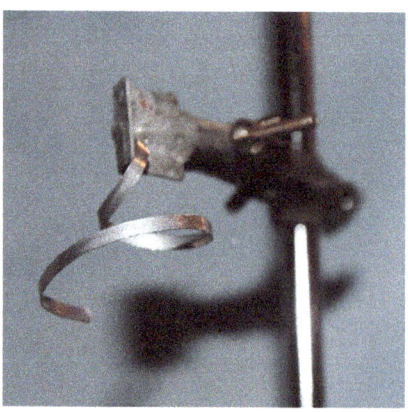

Corollary 11

DENSITY TOWER
Sabbath

SET UP: On the presentation table, you will need:

Filled test tubes in a test tube rack:

First set of test tubes in first rack and graduated cylinder are for Speaker 1:

    *Test tube 1 – 25 mL **red** **water***
    *Test tube 2 – 25 mL **yellow** **olive oil***
    *Test tube 3 – 25 mL **blue alcohol***
*First graduated cylinder – 35 mL **green** **corn syrup***

Second set of tests tubes in second rack and graduated cylinder are for Speaker 2:

    *Test tube 1 – 25 mL **red** **water***
    *Test tube 2 – 25 mL **yellow** **water***
    *Test tube 3 – 25 mL **blue** **water***
*Second graduated cylinder – 35 mL **green** **water***

This works best with two people participating, both speaking and performing the science demonstration.

Genesis 1:1 says, "In the beginning God created the heaven and the earth."

And when He got through creating this world,

and everything in it, Genesis 2:2 tells us,

He rested!

And gave us the wonderful,

blessed,

SABBATH!

And that's what we're going to talk about today.

When Jesus gave us the Sabbath, it was to give us rest,

And joy.

And it was to be a gift—just for us.

But for us to really enjoy it, He gave very good directions on how to best keep the Sabbath.

It is always important to know how to follow directions.

Jesus made one certain day for us to spend with Him for the Sabbath. Which day is that?

I am going let this green liquid be the seventh day.

Hold up graduated cylinder with green corn syrup in it.

You have to be very good at following directions. To get the right results, you must mix the solutions exactly according to the recipe. Sometimes I decide that I don't like to follow directions. I will just use whatever liquid I have handy. It might look the same. Some people say it doesn't matter which day we worship. One day seems exactly like another.

Hold up graduated cylinder with green water in it.

Next Jesus told us what time the Sabbath starts and stops. He said, "… from even unto even" (Lev. 23:32), which means from sunset to sunset. This red color will stand for being ready for the Sabbath when the sun goes down on Friday, the preparation day.

Density Tower ◆ 59

Carefully pour the test tube of red water slowly, running it down the inside surface of the cylinder to lessen the trauma of contact with the green syrup.

Sometimes we get so busy or distracted that we aren't ready for Sabbath in time on Friday evening.

Dump the red water into the cylinder.

Uh-oh, my cylinder doesn't look quite right.

Jesus also told us how to keep the Sabbath by turning away from doing work or our own selfish pleasures on His holy day. This yellow stands for leaving everyday activities alone on the Sabbath.

Add the olive oil in the same careful manner.

But I want to do what I want to do, when I want to do it. Why should I have to follow directions?

Add the yellow water quickly, and then look at it and make a face.

Oh, dear, this is starting to look really bad!

Our last color, blue, represents the benefits that come from spending this very special time with Jesus. If we follow His directions, we will enjoy all the blessings that He has promised.

Carefully add the alcohol and hold it up for all to see.

Well, here goes nothing!

Dump in the blue and hold up the results.

It looks like I didn't follow directions again and look what a mess I made. I surely can't enjoy this! What can I do?

There is nothing that will make your solution turn out right now. You'll just have to pour it out and start over.

But Jesus can make our lives right, if we ask Him to take us and make us willing to follow His directions.

And if we haven't followed His direction in our lives, we can certainly start over with His guidance.

Please bow your head with us. Lord Jesus, thank You for knowing that we need the rest and blessings of the Sabbath day.

And help us to keep it in the way that will bring us closest to You. Amen.

PREPARATION

Supplies:

1. Food coloring: bottles of red, yellow, blue, and green
2. Two test tube racks that hold at least three test tubes each
3. Six 25–30 mL test tubes
4. Two 100 mL graduated cylinders
5. Small container in which to mix corn syrup and food color
6. Small funnel to help pour corn syrup to bottom of cylinder without getting it on the sides
7. Water
8. Corn syrup
9. Olive oil
10. Isopropyl alcohol
11. Wooden skewer for mixing corn syrup

Directions:

1. The first set of test tubes and graduated cylinder are for Speaker 1.
2. Fill the test tubes and put them in the test tube rack (drop the color in each tube before filling).

   Test tube 1 - **Water** – four (4) drops of red food coloring

   Test tube 2 - **Olive oil**

   Test tube 3 - **Alcohol** – one (1) drop of blue food coloring

3. Fill the first graduated cylinder with 35 mL of premixed green syrup (one drop of color).

4. The second set of test tubes in the second rack are for Speaker 2:

   Test tube 1. **Water** with four (4) drops of red food coloring

   Test tube 2. **Water** with three (3) drops of yellow food coloring (adjust to match oil)

   Test tube 3. **Water** with one (1) drop of blue food coloring

5. Second graduated cylinder with 35 mL **water** and one drop of green food coloring

Illustrations:

COROLLARY 12

THE LONG DARK ROAD
The Balloon Without a Bang

SET UP: On presentation table, place a butane lighter and two balloons in bowls.

Let me tell you a story about a girl named "Cheryl." When Cheryl was about the age of some of you, she went to a school very much like the one you might attend. But it was a small school, with just two teachers.

Cheryl's teacher was named Ms. Lester, and the other teacher was her daddy!

One afternoon, about two o'clock, her daddy came to the classroom door, talked softly to Ms. Lester, then told Cheryl to get her things and come with him.

Now, her daddy didn't believe in missing school, so she wondered what was going on!

Daddy explained that "Mama" (that's what she called her Mother's mother) was in the hospital, and the doctors didn't think she would live very long.

A couple of hours later their clothes were packed, and they were ready to go.

After asking Jesus to take care of Mama and protect them

on the road, they started their trip from West Palm Beach, Florida, to Lucedale, Mississippi, over 700 miles away on narrow, two-lane roads.

When it got dark, Cheryl lay down in the back seat and went to sleep. (That was a long time ago, before most cars had seat belts.)

It seemed that she had just closed her eyes, but it turned out to be after midnight, when she was awakened by falling off the seat. They were stopped in the middle of the road. There were no lights anywhere, no houses, no stores, and no other cars. There was a deep drop-off on each side of the road.

Cheryl's daddy was outside the car, but when he got back in, he told them that the road was covered in wet oil and that it had caused the car to start spinning. It had turned around three times before he could stop it. They had a "thank you" prayer right then for the angels who must have been there to keep the car from going down one bank or the other.

Cheryl's daddy started driving again, though very slowly to make sure the road was not still slippery. Then he gradually sped up until they were going the speed limit, 55 mph.

Cheryl was just falling asleep again when Daddy stopped the car and got out. Again, there were no lights in sight.

She sat up just as Daddy stuck his head in the window. He said,

"I thought we had a flat tire, and the front left is flat – but the front right is going flat too; and, of course, we only have one spare! I'm going to change the left one, and we'll just try to limp along until we can find a service station open. But we haven't seen a station, a house, or even another car in the last half hour, and it is past midnight!"

The Long, Dark Road; the Balloon without a Bang ◆ 65

As he went back to change the tire, Cheryl could tell that her mother was crying softly.

She remembered that they had prayed for help and safety for the trip.

She remembered that they asked Jesus to take care of Mama.

She knelt down in the back seat and prayed again.

Then she leaned over the front seat and said, "Don't worry, Mommy, I asked Jesus to send His angel to blow up the tire with his own breath and hold it with his own finger, and to keep Mama safe till we get there."

Daddy got back in the car and said he had done all he could. He changed the flat tire, but he could hear the air escaping from the other one.

They started slowly on up the road—that long, dark road. Daddy said the steering was hard at first, but it seemed to get easier and easier. Soon they were back up to the speed limit.

Almost an hour passed before they came to an open gas station and pulled in.

As Daddy got out and walked around the car, he heard "spsss," and he watched as the tire went from full to flat, right before his eyes!

When the station attendant had removed the tire, he called Daddy over and showed him. There was a hole in the tire so big he could stick two fingers through it.

When they made it to the hospital, Mama was doing much better. She lived many more happy years, and Cheryl learned that Jesus cares about girls and boys, and He answers prayers.

66 ◆ *Designer Science*

There was AIR UNDER PRESSURE in that tire, so what should have happened when the tire got a hole in it?

Wait for answers.

Here we have two balloons with air under pressure. What will happen if I put a flame to one of them?

Lift the balloon without water from its bowl. Wait for answers, and then apply the flame to the bottom of the balloon. When it goes, "POP!" discuss what happened.

Okay, let's try again on this balloon. Will it pop too?

Lift the water balloon. Wait for answers. Some might notice the water and figure it out; some won't. Let them discuss what will happen for a moment. Then apply the flame to the bottom. (Be sure not to accidentally put the flame to a part of balloon not cooled by water! Don't hold it there too long.

Why didn't it pop?

The water absorbed and disbursed the heat of the flame, keeping the latex below its melting point.

But why didn't THE TIRE go flat? That was an answer to prayer.

The Long, Dark Road; the Balloon without a Bang ♦ 67

PREPARATION

Supplies:

1. Two dark colored 12-inch latex balloons, plus extras in case of breakage
2. 11-inch butane lighter
3. Two bowls large enough to hold a balloon each

Directions:

1. The opaquer the balloons are, the more the water is hidden.
2. Fill one balloon with water until it runs over the top, then finish blowing it up with air. (The more water you get in the balloon, the more heat can be absorbed in your demonstration.)
3. Inflate the balloons only about $2/3$ full.
4. Practice heating without popping because different brands of balloons behave differently.

Corollary 13

I CAN SEE CLEARLY
Baptism

SET UP: On presentation table place: a 1000 mL beaker with a premixed solution of water and phenolphthalein; a 125 mL flask of vinegar; and a 50 mL beaker of ammonia.

We all have sin in our lives. The Bible says, in Romans 3:23, "All have sinned."

And that's pretty scary, because Romans 6:23 says, "When you sin the pay you get is death" (*New International Reader's Version*).

And that is talking about eternal death!

I don't want to die at all—and especially not that death! What can I do about it?

That is what Nicodemus and Jesus were talking about when they met secretly one night. Jesus told him that he had to be born again.

Well that's just fine! How do I go about being BORN now that I am old?

Nicodemus asked that also. Then Jesus told him he needed to be born of water and the Spirit—that means being baptized and filled with the Holy Spirit.

But Jesus didn't just tell us ABOUT baptism, He showed us.

It was at the very beginning of His time of formal ministry at age thirty. He went and found His cousin, John, who was at the river Jordan, and asked to be baptized.

Although they had never met, John recognized Him as the Son of God, and, at first, he refused. He felt totally unworthy to baptize Him.

But Jesus insisted—even though He had no sin to wash away—for He knew that someday you must decide to be baptized. His life must be a complete pattern for you to follow.

In Mark 16:16, Jesus puts believing and being baptized together. He says, "He who believes and is baptized will be saved; but he who does not believe will be condemned" (NKJV).

So being baptized is an acknowledgement of your belief. It is like saying, "I am willing to tell the world that I believe in Jesus."

But, is it necessary to be baptized?

Well, when John hesitated to baptize Jesus, we are told, "Jesus answered him, 'This is the way it HAS to be now. This is the PROPER way to do EVERYTHING that GOD REQUIRES of us.' Then John gave in to Him" (Matt. 3:15, God's Word).

Acts 22:16, in *The Message*, says, "So what are you waiting for? GET UP AND GET YOURSELF BAPTIZED— scrubbed clean of those sins and personally acquainted with God."

Here I have a large beaker of pure, crystal clear water.

Hold up the large beaker.

This water represents us when we have not sinned. But the verse says that all of us have sinned, so we have to add THIS clear liquid, which we will call sin.

Pour the ammonia from the small beaker into the large beaker.

Look what happens to our lives when sin enters. It isn't pure and crystal clear anymore!

Comment on the fact that it is kind of a pretty color now, and sometimes sin looks pretty and attractive at first.

But now, how do we get rid of the sin that has entered our lives?

Like the verse said— "scrubbed clean" through baptism.

Pour in the vinegar from the flask and swish large beaker around slightly.

Of course, there will be temptations and sin after you are baptized, but you don't have to be baptized again each time you sin. You just come with repentance and seek forgiveness, and Jesus cleanses you again.

Remember that verse we read at the beginning that says, "When you sin the pay you get is death"? Well, the rest of the verse is: "But God gives you the gift of eternal life. That's because of what Christ Jesus our Lord has done."

I Can See Clearly, Baptism ♦ 71

PREPARATION

Supplies:

1. Distilled water (In an emergency, you might find yourself using tap water, which could be slightly basic, lending a pinkish hue to your water to begin with. If this happens, drop vinegar into your beaker of water, a drop at a time, until it just becomes colorless. Be careful, too much vinegar will negate the rest of the demonstration.)
2. Household ammonia
3. White vinegar
4. Phenolphthalein (1%)
5. 1000 mL beaker
6. 125 mL flask
7. 50 mL beaker
8. Medicine dropper

Directions:

1. Premix 30 drops of phenolphthalein in 700 mL of distilled H_2O in a 1000 mL beaker.
2. Pour 125 mL of vinegar into a 125 mL flask.
3. Pour 30 mL ammonia into a 50 mL beaker.

TEACH Services, Inc.
P U B L I S H I N G

We invite you to view the complete
selection of titles we publish at:
www.TEACHServices.com

We encourage you to write us
with your thoughts about this,
or any other book we publish at:
info@TEACHServices.com

TEACH Services' titles may be purchased in
bulk quantities for educational, fund-raising,
business, or promotional use.
bulksales@TEACHServices.com

Finally, if you are interested in seeing
your own book in print, please contact us at:
publishing@TEACHServices.com

We are happy to review your manuscript at no charge.

www.ingramcontent.com/pod-product-compliance
Lightning Source LLC
Chambersburg PA
CBHW042133160426
43199CB00021B/2905